Penguin Modern European Poets
Advisory Editor: A. Alvarez

Three Painter-Poets: Arp, Schw

Jean (Hans) Arp was born in 1887 in A[illegible] studied in Paris. In Zurich in 1916 he was one of the co-founders of Dada, and later, after settling in France, he became a Surrealist. He died in 1966.

Kurt Schwitters (1887–1948) was a poet and abstract painter best known as the inventor of Merz, a form of Dada. In 1929 he first visited Norway, and in 1937 he emigrated there. In 1940 he escaped from Norway and came to Britain, where he died.

Paul Klee was born in 1879 and was a Swiss painter and etcher. He was trained at Munich and spent many years teaching at the Düsseldorf Academy. From the 1920s he was famous, and over a hundred of his works were confiscated from German galleries by the Nazis. He died in 1940.

Three Painter-Poets
Arp, Schwitters, Klee

Selected Poems

Translated with an introduction by
Harriett Watts

Penguin Books

Penguin Books Ltd, Harmondsworth,
Middlesex, England
Penguin Books Inc., 7110 Ambassador Road,
Baltimore, Maryland 21207, U.S.A.
Penguin Books Australia Ltd, Ringwood,
Victoria, Australia
Penguin Books Canada Ltd,
41 Steelcase Road West, Markham, Ontario, Canada

First published 1974

Made and printed in Great Britain by
Cox & Wyman Ltd,
London, Reading and Fakenham
Set in Monotype Bembo

Contents

PAUL KLEE (*1879–1940*)

Acknowledgements

For permission to publish translations of Hans Arp's poems, from the original-language copyright holders, included in *Gesammelte Gedichte I*, grateful acknowledgement is due to Limes Verlag, Wiesbaden, and Verlag der Arche, Zurich.

For permission to publish translations of poems by Kurt Schwitters and Paul Klee, from the original-language copyright holders, included in Kurt Schwitters, *Anna Blume und Ich*, and *Paul Klee, Gedichte*, ed. Felix Klee, grateful acknowledgement is due to Verlag der Arche, Zurich.

A number of the Hans Arp translations were published in *Delos*, *Antaeus*, *Literary Review*, and *These Are Also Wings*.

Introduction

The painter-poet is an intriguing phenomenon among creative personalities. Seldom is he equally recognized in both spheres. The three artists included in this volume, Hans Arp, Kurt Schwitters and Paul Klee, are all better known as painters than as writers. Yet each was a poet of considerable talent and originality. To those who know Arp, Schwitters and Klee only as painters this selection of poems should reveal new aspects of their talents.

The bilingual Alsatian Hans Arp, sculptor, painter and poet, wrote in both German and French. Many of the poems in this selection appeared in some preliminary version at the time when Arp was a central figure in the Dada movement which had originated in Zurich in 1916. Arp's contribution to Dada can in no way be dismissed as nihilistic – a facile criticism often levelled at the movement – or as merely high-spirited pranks intended to unnerve a well-padded, placid bourgeoisie. Rooted in the German romantic tradition and attracted to such mystic philosophers as Jacob Böhme, Arp retains the romantic vocabulary of fairy-tales and of man's union with nature. After radical transposition, it is this vocabulary that emerges revitalized in his poetry and in the rationale he offers of his own artistic development and pre-occupations.

In a journal of the years 1914–54, *Our Daily Dream*, Arp offers a delightfully untheoretical presentation of his aesthetic theories, and he comments often on the intense moment of Zurich Dada. Arp was the first of the Dadaists to proclaim 'das Gesetz des Zufalls', the law of the accident as a new basis for artistic creation. His work he describes as 'ordered according to the law of the accident, the accident which, to me, is but an element of the inexplicable reason, the incomprehensible order by which nature herself is governed'. Dada, according to Arp, was in the deepest sense constructive, rather than destructive. 'Dada is the primal source of all art. Dada is for the "without sense" of art, which is not to say non-sense. Dada is without sense like nature. Dada is for nature and against art. Dada is direct like nature and tries to find for each thing its real place.' In his desire to find a new basis for creation far removed from human reason and its attempt to imitate nature, Arp turned to what he called 'concrete art', an art that would no longer copy nature but could produce as directly as the tree, which each year brings forth its fruit:

> Concrete art wishes to transform the world and make it more bearable. It would release mankind from the most dangerous madness, that of vanity, and simplify the life of men. It would integrate man's life into nature. Reason uproots man and imposes on him a tragic existence. Concrete art, however, is an elemental, healthy, natural art which permits the stars of peace, love and poetry to bloom in the hearts and heads of men. Wherever concrete art steps in, melancholy has to leave, taking with it its grey suitcases filled with black sighs.

Arp's rejection of 'reason' as the basis for ordering a work of art is most obvious in his poetry. Words and phrases meet, not in the interest of semantic 'message' or logical coherence, but on terms of non-logical associative qualities in language. Often the words seem to be generated by a sound-sequence that has managed to establish itself, quite without Arp's having consciously willed it. An example is to be found in 'two little arabs, adult and arabesque' in which the *p*s, *pum*s and *pom*s dominating a stanza of Arp's French and German versions take over an English translation as well:

> whereupon they felt themselves most rococo

like pompeian pumpworkers
that pump the pompadour on the gold-leafed pump
from their cute little rumps they let fly giant
balloon baskets made of skin
with great wild star eyes
which were shod in parchment shoes
and topped with polished agate hats

Arp delights in breaking into accustomed verbal associations, jumbling up the dismantled elements and then reassembling them into startling new word-constellations. He was particularly adroit at re-aligning elements of clichés, figures of speech and German compound words. Often he takes an expression literally, letting it fall apart at its figurative seams, or he splits it acoustically with a pun, meanwhile rejoining the exposed parts into new combinations, a transformed context in which the old semantic elements – with all associations bared – can never be the same again. In this manner words are stripped of their 'sense', but in the place of normal sense Arp unleashes energies of poetic association which semantic bonds had previously checked.

In the Journal one finds a short passage, 'Regenpagoden nach Regenpagoden, die Beine nach oben den Kopf nach unten, stürzen aus Wolken nieder.' A rough English translation would read: 'Rain-pagodas upon rain-pagodas, legs up heads down, plunge down from the clouds.' First, the compound word 'Regen*bogen*' (rainbows) has been transposed acoustically into 'Regen*pagoden*'. All one's habitual storm expectations are thwarted. The downpour of evoked rainbows alone, rather than the accustomed raindrops, is surprising enough an image. But here we are confronted by a pagoda-torrent, embodied pagodas with heads and legs, and up-ended pagodas to boot. The resulting image is not strung together on any logical thread, but one can nevertheless trace the lines of verbal play in the new constellation.

Although Arp was often to divide and recombine phrases and compound words, he did not reduce language beyond the limit of the simple word. What he did was tap the associative powers of the word, left untouched, in word combinations intended solely to express semantic 'meaning'. He rarely tampered with accepted grammatical patterns and his syntax is relatively simple and straightforward.

Arp's vocabulary and images can often be traced to the German 'Märchen'; he restores a lost sense of wonder to jaded elements through fantastic new combinations. Objects from nature play an important role in his work: clouds, water, plants, flowers, animals, stones, jewels, stars. Arp's universe is remarkably fecund, filled with navels, eggs, umbilical cords, populated by the unpredictable offspring of unprecedented pairings. His poems, sculptures and paintings seem to have grown organically into their final states. Indeed, the final state scarcely existed for Arp. Repeatedly Arp returns to a text, elaborating on it each time in a new series of variations. His translations of his own poems from French into German or vice versa often vary greatly from one version to another, depending upon the possibilities for word-play and improvisation which the second language had to offer. His sculptures, paintings and collages are a continuation of the same fertile, organic world evoked by his poetry.

A painter-poet with whom Arp collaborated in the 1920s was the Hannover artist Kurt Schwitters. In 1918 Schwitters sought entrance to the Berlin Klub-Dada but was rejected by Richard Huelsenbeck as being insufficiently political. Arp, who in 1920 visited the International Dada Fair in Berlin with Max Ernst, had little to do with the new, politically oriented Dada, but he immediately took up contact with Schwitters and worked closely with him for the next ten years. Schwitters, excluded from orthodox Dada, had already started his own movement – 'Merz'. With his ever-present sense of humour, in his insistence on the need to abolish boundaries between the arts and between art and life itself, Schwitters exemplified the spirit of Dada at its inception in Zurich.

The Schwitters coinage 'Merz', a word-fragment with no prior signification, was lifted from the name of a Hannover Bank, 'Kommerz und Privat Bank'. In Arp's poems language is not broken down beyond the unit of the word. Schwitters carries the process of reduction much further, declaring that the primary units of construction in poetry are letters and syllables, as well as words and sentences. His earliest poems, still under the influence of German expressionism, take as their model the poet August Stramm, an expressionist who disrupted in particular the established behaviour patterns of the German verb. Schwitters continues with the same defiance of grammatical rules and lets the verb run rampant. Nouns, adjectives, adverbs become verbs; infinitives, that were never before nominative, usurp the place of nouns. Conjugated verbs stand alone, with no easily discernible subject. A third person suddenly finds itself with a second- or first-person conjugation. Even while under the influence of expressionism, Schwitters is pursuing his personal track of questioning the accepted units, rules and materials of artistic creation. Grammar was but the first convention to crumble in his wake.

As Schwitters moved into his 'Merz period', his poetry began to assume the characteristics one associates with his collages. Any material was admissible to the collage. All material was of equal value: there was no such thing as matter unsuitable for a work of art. What counted was how each element stood in relation to every other element in the work. It was this relationship alone that gave the elements their value. Schwitters explained, 'In Merz painting the box-lid, the playing-card, the newspaper clipping turns into surface; a string, the stroke of a brush or a pencil, into line; wire-gauze, a repainted surface, pasted on sandwich wrapping paper, into lapislazuli; cotton wads, into softness.' Likewise, in Merz poetry, the given elements were 'whole sentences from newspapers, posters, catalogues, discussions, etc., with and without alteration'. Banality was of no aesthetic consideration in determining what verbal elements would be lifted from their public context for relocation in a Schwitters poem. Certain official announcements, in Schwitters's variation, illustrate his alteration of elements one is accustomed to seeing in such public notices:

> Do not open until
> the train is in motion.
>
> This seat reserved for
> unhandicapped dogs.

In this collection, the prose poem 'The Onion' is perhaps the best example of Schwitters's Merz vocabulary, with words and slogans taken straight from everyday life and no attempt made at aesthetic refinement. All effect derives from the juxtaposition of verbal elements, from interpolation of these public formulas into the mad plot line of a man who supervises his own butchering and subsequent reconstruction. (Fortunately, for the reassembled happy ending, the butchers hadn't gone so far as to grind him up into sausage-meat.) Schwitters also throws in several of his expressionist verb manoeuvres for good measure.

Whereas Arp's creations give an impression of organic growth into a natural unit, Schwitters's paintings and poems are the product of a forced juxtaposition of alien elements that constitute an arbitrary harmony existing solely in terms of their relation to one another within the work itself.

At the same time as he was constructing his verbal Merz collages, Schwitters began to experiment with what later came to be called concrete poetry. Included in this selection are two alphabet poems and a letter picture poem. A printer and ad-man by profession, Schwitters was able to apply the skills of his trade to develop new types and type-settings for his poems and the various Merz journals he published. Isolated letters were not his only reduced units for poetry. He also composed number poems, with carefully constructed, visual arrangements of numerical sequences. And he did not stop at the visual, concrete presentation of poetry. A long poem from 1921, which he considered one of his most important, was a sound poem – 'The Sonata in Primal Sounds'. A short, printed reproduction of a passage from the 'Ursonata' serves only to whet one's curiosity as to what it must have actually sounded like with Schwitters himself performing it. Apparently almost every performance transformed an audience of scoffers – from generals and society dames to students and workers – into boisterous enthusiasts:

Lanke trr gll
  pe pe pe pe pe
    ooka ooka ooka ooka

Lanke trr gll
  pii pii pii pii pii
    Züüka züüka züüka züüka

Lanke trr gll
  Rrmmp
  Rrnnf
Lanke trr gll

Perhaps more immediately accessible is his sneeze scherzo from 1945:

TESCH
TSCHIA
HAICH
TSCHIA
HAISCH
HAPPA ISH
HAPPA PEPPA ISH
HAPPA PEPPA ISCH
HAPPA PEPPA ISCH
HAPPA PEPPE TSCHAA!

Schwitters was by far the most wide-ranging experimenter of the three artists represented in this volume. He was totally consistent in his demand that the old aesthetic categories be removed, that there was no material inadmissable to the work of art, that there was no containing a work of art within the limits of genre. In his own performance he proved that no such boundaries need exist. One final comment on Schwitters's openness to all experience as raw material for creation, on his humorous, enthusiastic acceptance of life's carnival fare might be provided by a poem he himself wrote in English:

Dada ist eine Hypothese

Motto: I think the world's menagerie
the greatest kind of show,
that anyone could wish to see
wherever they may go,
t'will be a pleasant task to me
to introduce to you
the different sorts of animals
you'll find are here on view.
First come, first served.

The third artist in this volume, Paul Klee, was not a participant in the Dada movement, even though Arp, in particular, recognized in Klee's work a sense of irony and play akin to the spirit of Dada. His written work, however, cannot be considered 'experimental' in terms of the no-holds-barred operations Schwitters and Arp were carrying out on language. He is probably the least known of the three as a writer. But not only was Klee a poet, he was an accomplished musician as well, and an astute musical critic. Although Klee decided at about the age of twenty against a career as a professional violinist, he continued to play with orchestras, often as soloist, and in chamber groups. His writings are largely contained in a diary of the years 1898–1918, edited and published by his son Felix Klee in 1956. The diary, which no one saw during Klee's lifetime, is composed of day-by-day entries, many of which Klee rewrote several times before including the revised versions in a final draft. These private texts that Klee left posterity seem dictated by the same instinct for intricate balance that one associates with Klee's paintings. The diary is interwoven with accounts of all Klee's interests: reflections on his own personal development and his progress as an artist, comments on music – concerts, musicians, his own performances, critical reactions to authors he was reading, and impressions from everyday life, rendered occasionally as poems, but presented more often in a prose that rhythmically converts easily into verse. The diary, candid, yet cool and objective, is witness to Klee's unrelenting scrutiny of his own consciousness and aesthetic sensibility.

It is fitting that the main source for Felix Klee's one volume of his father's collected poems, poems so often characterized by a critical self-consciousness, should be a diary. On occasion, this self-consciousness might seem to teeter on the verge of sentimentality, which must then be countered with an appropriate measure of irony. This interplay can, at times, leave a tinge of preciousness about some of Klee's poems, in which the delicate balance struck may seem a bit too delicate, or even trivial, to some palates. Yet this problem was a fundamental one that Klee had to confront as an artist. His poems, like many of his paintings, must succeed as miniatures: fleet, brilliant, with incredible economy, concentration, technical virtuosity. When one of these poems 'works', it is an epiphany, graceful, scintillating and, in the same breath, profound.

The mathematical precision of Klee's engravings and drawings is present in his verse, each poem achieved with extreme economy of means, one line in place of a verbose paragraph. Titles given to certain paintings illustrate Klee's evocative concentration:

'Simplex visits Complex', 'Silver-moon-mould-blossom', 'Abandoned site of an exotic city – as landmark, a tomato', 'The attack as symbol, will and fulfilment'.

Like Arp's inventive titles, which were often organic extensions of his visual work, Klee's titles serve as further crystallization of his paintings.

The harmony and balance achieved by Klee was analysed by the linguist Roman Jakobson as the result of a dialectical process. Klee himself dissected the balance he was trying to attain in painting:

Well-composed pictures give the impression of a consummate harmony. An illusion, however, if the layman assumes that one arrives at this all-encompassing harmony by construction on the basis of harmonizing the elements one by one. Such a process has a feeble impact. For the first part, having been brought into harmony with the second part, does not demand a third part. Only when one and one stand in head-on opposition is number three necessary, emerging to resolve this confrontation into harmony. This new, three-part harmony then convinces all the more forcefully.

This intricate balance of odds against evens often lends an aphoristic sting to Klee's poems and reflects their inherent dialectical structure. It also seems to reflect the three talents Klee was able to harmonize within the entirety of his artistic production. One short diary entry from Tunisia in 1916 illustrates again the poet Klee's visual and musical acuity. An unerring sense of composition, with detail, colour, tone and line recorded in elegant economy, succeeds in re-creating a street scene most vividly:

> High notes of the oboe, tambourine beats, enticing one to the theatre of snake-charmer and scorpion-swallower. An exquisite street show. The donkey also looks on.

There are no particular problems to be mentioned in connection with the translation of Klee. These English versions are much more 'literal' than those of Arp and Schwitters. With Arp and Schwitters, I often had to seek a non-literal English equivalent that could reproduce, or attempt to reproduce, the sort of verbal play that had taken place in German. I should like especially to thank Christopher Middleton and Rosmarie Waldrop for their most helpful criticism and suggestions in solving some of the tricky problems of translation posed by Schwitters and Arp.

HARRIETT WATTS

Hans Arp *(1887-1965)*

*

the nightbirds carry burning lanterns in the beams of their eyes. they steer delicate ghosts and ride on wagons with delicate veins.

the black wagon is harnessed to the mountain.

the black bell is harnessed to the mountain.

the black rocking-horse is harnessed to the mountain.

the dead bring saws and tree-trunks along to the pier.

the harvest falls from the maws of birds onto the iron threshing-floors.

the angels land in baskets of air.

the fish take up their walking sticks and roll in the stars towards the exit.

*

black winds hang like chains from the stars.
grappling irons attack black lacquered walls.
the maps of the cities glow.
the houses run on seven rubies or spin like tops on diamonds.
thunder-claps roll through the vast courtyards and the queens are toppling from milk stools.
from the necks of the earth climb the tenants and sub-tenants with their galvanized spiders.
out of the glue come little glass skeletons tolling like chaos.
who will bear up our little coffin beneath the cool morning star.

*

laughing beasts foam out of iron tankards.
cloud barrels drive the animals out of their seeds and stones.
hoofs stand naked on stone-aged stones still as a mouse beside twigs and fishbones.
antlers spear snowballs.
the kings gallop on chairs into the mountains and preach the december horn: lower straw bridges deliver iron letters soundless and easily audible.
turtle doves freeze in the ice bottle.

*

interwound boys blow the wonder horn.
angels in golden shoes empty sacks of red rocks into every joint.
masts and constellations are already forming.
the sisters point out the tracks of air-castles money-belts orphans steamed cow morsels saddled hares newly upholstered lions.
on flaming spokes the birds roll across the heavens.
man and mouse swim drunken on soft fingers.
stars sneeze flower gardens out of their wax noses.
blazing lions whiz over the quivering birch trees.
everyone with a tail ties on a lantern the whole night long is stood on its head danced astride dragons greased pole climbing and corporeal boxing fill the night with bow-wow.

*

immense hour-glasses filled with stars are reversed.
in subterranean corridors there are throngs of black flowers and crystalline coffins.
heraldic beasts at a gallop race for the horizon.
great white hares drink from white lava streams.
he sees also the seas hanging perpendicular like mirrors in mountains but does not flee with the amateur rabble into the arches.
he reaps the snow harvest.
he weighs the snow anchor and from the giant bird's blood he fells crystals of flesh and of blood.

*

solemnly the noblewoman pumps clouds into sacks of leather and stone.

soundlessly the giant cranes hoist trilling larks into the sky.

the sand-castles are stuffed with cotton-wool dolls.

the ammonites discuses and millstones stand awed in the locks.

the ships are called hansel and gretel and oblivious they sail on.

the dragon wears the inscription kunigunda and is led on a leash.

the feet are sawed off the cities the church spires allowed only complete freedom of movement in the cellars therefore neither are we required to polish the claws the horns and the weathercocks.

*

in january it snows graphite in the goat pelt.
in february there appears the bouquet of chalk-white light and white stars.
in march the avenging angel mates and the bricks and the moths flutter forth and the stars rock in their rings and the wind-breaker blossoms rustle on their chains and the princesses sing in their fog-pots.
who hurries on little fingers and wings after the winds of morning.

*

the seraphim and cherubim climb up and down the white construction ladders and don't know the reason why.

the mighty beasts stalk on wadding balls. they sift red hot coals onto the beds fling spears at the feathered humps and heap stones on top of the horny signposts.

the children put on their death-boots and wait for the time which crumbles away in little black toboggans red-jawed chapters and pious stopped clocks and wait for the cosmetic lion with the tail of fine wire full of tiny knots.

in the lounge-chairs of shadow sit the calcified dead. they clap their hands and bark.

giant birds bell in the wooded gorge.

no one detects now the track of his baby shoes. they left not even a threadlike trace of a tiny hiking-song in the air.

the pistils fall from the stars. the stars are rapt in their aviaries.

the stars split in two and spit booby-traps. the muscles in the stars rip apart.

the boneless princes stream like pulp around the wheels of midnight.

but in the metal tent there sits the giantess iron-head with the iron pot on her iron head with the false calves the pillar of advertisements and the owl. the giantess crams her smoke pipe her stove pipe onto her head bows and speaks merrily merrily merrily.

all at once the globe becomes transparent and floating there as if in a fishbowl are the magistri horti deliciarum.

the world gates bang open and shut.
the wax-doll time melts.
incessantly the super-void the harmony egg bombards.

*

when it burns before the harps and freezes behind the
easels
when the leather hare stands like Venice up to its knees in
water
when the pyramids polish their glassy horse-blinkers with
mortal soft-boiled leftovers
a wowl is the ultimate substance

when the tears are covered with unwrinkled lids
when the sirloin-tipped shoes are worn to the bone-pope
when the free-hand sketcher with bones jutting out
sketches the stemless egg
a wowl is the ultimate substance

when the cohorts in sin harrow with the purgatorial
mops
when the allahs all trill like larks
when the four-cornered buttoned-up suns roll on
helter-skelter with a whoa and a giddy-up
a wowl is the ultimate substance

*

god is native to stove-pipe hats
from the ears of the stars fall atheistic roses
what else would fall from the crust of the years

on my golden bough I wear a wedding ring
a wedding ring consists of a wreath of air and a point of
   light
among the public bodies I alone wear a wedding ring

my lower length of a head falls asleep
my fire is cooked

on the uppermost branch of the tower live the mouthless
   crates
the earless casks
the eyeless sacks
the five-sensed paper bags

no no they will never again fly hence
the road comes to a stop under their feet
they are tugged from in front
bumped from behind
held from above
borne from beneath
just like the brothers once upon a time long long ago

from my furnished ceiling falls a rock of petrus
from a well-furnished ceiling hang new-fledged stars
   carbolic aquariums and rocks of petrus

the eyes of my bolster are closed forever
my woodwork-vices are full of eggs

*

cautiously the sphinxes poke their noses out of the rind
because mister string brings the rope
and mister rope brings the string
to tie up the sack full of papal bull-moths

the bones grow faster and faster in the rocks
the kisses fester in the foundations
the eyes are no longer fastened to the shoes
the vases sigh like diamonds

if to this happy holiday one stitches a cackling bouquet
it turns into a head
that regards itself at once in the mirror
and asks itself is it me or not
the folded gloves ask themselves the same
whenever their comfortable tongues pronounce the
  following prayer
go upwards and push downwards
go downwards and push upwards
go forwards and push backwards
go backwards and push forwards
go right and push left
go left and push right

therefore one should best remove the hats from the masts
  and other crosses
the interior ties from the necks
the celibate eggs from the arcs of triumph
and lay them once more on the creation table

set the little laurel-wreathed quarter hours on their
ephemerid chairs
and order the creation table and the ephemerid chairs in
the strict form of an interim pretzel
then abandon one's shoes with the utmost dispatch
and relinquish the rest to the final eel with crop damage
gratis still to come

*

I have rolled from one beginning to another
and have found no end
and have rolled from one end to the other
and have found no beginning
therefore I remain seated on my big toe

these are no empty diphthong kisses and theresian tin-pan alley tirades
in which peloponized stove-pipes are clapped down over exiled bones
why else would the wheels have put on stockings

the secret feather will never go off

already the tones with faded walls have hopped away
and the vagrant stars on the beggar's leash have fallen asleep

the secret feather will never go off
even if we wait for a thousand pines
a pine tree has three hundred sixty-five branches

even y gomez sala has leapt over the meat-acre
on a cavalier's shoe a monoped and a centipede

therefore I remain seated on my big toe
and laugh to shake my contents well before using

*

two little arabs adult and arabesque
played on two little hobby-horse fiddles
all at once a pipe appeared
to the two little arabs adult and arabesque
a tobacco pipe on doll's feet
at such moments points fall on our points
fat like metrical apples

but the two little arabs adult and arabesque
sneezed rather than shivered
like courageous turtles who have lost their shells
sneeze rather than shiver
they sneezed with such might
that their little hobby-horse fiddles went sailing
into a far but musical land

hereupon they were enticed by a half-filled glass of wine
that was halfway on its way
whose endless end ended in a bald sea
which was covered with an oil cloth
the two little arabs adult and arabesque
questioned the pipe about the half-full glass of wine

'the wine is mine'
replied the pipe with firmness
but continued in a juicy voice
'gorblimey gorblemony gorblorangey
drink it just the same
it is part of a still-life
indeed I might well say of a deadstill still-life
that was beginning on its way
whose endless end as everyone knows ends in a bald sea'

the two little arabs adult and arabesque
like two omnivorous pyramids drained
this glass half filled with wine
and devoured in addition
a box of matches three pears and an apple

whereupon they felt themselves most rococo
like pompeian pumpworkers
that pump the pompadour on the gold-leafed pump
from their cute little rumps they let fly giant
balloonbaskets made of skin
with great wild star eyes
which were shod in parchment shoes
and topped with polished agate hats
thereupon the two little arabs adult and arabesque
lost their cool completely
bombarded the nightingale
which struck up the alarm clocks on the porcelain
hills of the still and natural lives
with newborn four-footed stones
and then they vanished
into the aromatic arabian arumperfumeral night

*

next in line were the cluckcluckers
they laughed tears of damascus
reproduced as is proper in a flower-pot
and refused to fall for chintzy mummy-tits
at a moment's notice they could let bits of wisdom
flow unmilked from their udder hats
but chose instead to say cluckcluck
and were right
for it hit the nail on the head
and moreover still came from the heart

but as they began to dream inveterately into the blue
scales the size of roof tiles fell from their eyes
and in such profusion
that they would have covered the leaves of all forests
as a result
they soon resembled the innocent plants
addicted to calligraphy
and although they wrapped themselves in shadow
there was nothing more there that was cosily munching
  and crunching

and now as the ticktockers came climbing over them
  from behind
they said for the last time cluckcluck
whereupon the ticktockers screamed ticktock with all
  their might
and in fact without stop
for not one was a man of few words
they were wound up instead like a child's mechanical toy
  by wind-up-ticktockers

who were wound up in turn by wind-up-ticktocker-
winder-ups
and so forth all the way back to the first cause

for the ticktockers life had but one meaning
and that was to ticktock
they ticktocked until their compression-springs sprang
the sprung springs without exception were laid out
in honour in gigantic iceboxes
often world-famous award-winning ticktockers were
present
on tasty display like titbits in a gourmet shop-window
when they once by mistake said tucktuck
everyone including their wind-up-ticktockers
refused to hear more of progressive ticktocking
and lapsed into the reverse namely retardation
ever more slowly ever less often they said tucktuck
until one day they sank speechless

now came the respectable clackclackers
leaping out of the cedar-chests
they clackclacked within decent bounds
and chased away an unchaste fish-god
who offered them rosy nude girls
they demolished his flock-folds
clackclack thundered from their cavernous mouths

and as the fish-god was a foreigner
his rights as a guest were abused
and soon he departed
gurgling like a phosphorescent shipshape sea-monster
the ship on top the shape below
floating down the rhine

the day skeleton

1

the eyes converse like flames on waves
the eyes would like to withdraw from the days
the flames have no name
each flame has five fingers
the hands caress the wings in the sky

2

out of the words the lips emerge
like beauty from the waves of the day
beauty is embraced by light
like the bell by kisses

3

but what has come in its place
the wings fall from the peak of the table
like earthen leaves
before the lips
night is entrenched in the wings
and the singing chains are no longer there
between the wings
the skeleton of light empties the fruits
the body of kisses will never awaken
it was never real
the sea of the wings rocks these tears
the bell speaks with the head
and the fingers lead us through the fields of air
to the nests of the eyes

where the names perish
but what has come in its place
in the height of the sky
neither sleep nor wakefulness
for the graves are brighter than the days

4

a singing sky is arched about the heart
yet we cannot believe its songs
in vain the fruits flourish
weeping the eyes look
to the rims of the days
the days are nothing but wounds
the lips kiss into emptiness
the sun sheds its leaves
the leaves cover the eyes
the light is hollow
ashes have covered the pasture of wings

5

beneath the leaves the flames fall asleep
the leaf of the sky is blue
green birds cradle themselves in the branches
you will hear them singing the whole of may
from the meadows of lips appear the eyeless flowers
the ground becomes aware of itself for the voice
approaches
the leaf of my heart turns black
my eyes have become black fruits
the breast of the light caves in
but in the summer the dead once again grow wings

6

with closed eyes I grope my
way through the brightness
the light releases itself from the day
and the wings visit the lips
between sky and tongue grows the golden weight
the burning flesh of the sky plunges down over the
  earth
the fruits are drumming like fists against the ground
the days bear fire on their waves
the sky is a blazing wing
immense the roar of the summer fruits

7

where are the leaves
the bells have withered
it no longer rings upon earth
where once we walked
the light is in shreds
the tracks of the wings lead into emptiness
where are the lips
where are the eyes
hideous their heart shattered between the heads
the last breath drops like a stone from the bodies
where once we spoke blood now runs from the fire
and the formless wreath turns over in the black ground
forever invisible the beautiful earth
the wings no longer hover about us

8

the flames feed death
the day coos so terribly

tongue is laid out by tongue
the air is full of wounds
in the wounds the shadows nest
who plucks the leaf of the sky
the trees are dead
the light is scarred
only in sleep is the sky filled with eyes and with buds
only in sleep do the wings cast no shadows on the
lights of the eyes
and the songs wander with waves and clouds
yet such years survive no longer than days

9

the leaves rush to the aid of the wings
the bells are on the wrong track
far higher than the clouds of the eyes
float the hearts and the blissful fruits
before the leaf has opened his eye
the fire has already bathed
the wings carry the sky
the words recede from the mouth like smoke

10

the eyes are wreaths of earth
the voices can only be heard from leaf to leaf
when the eyes melt the light ripens
and falls like a bell into beautiful days
and the nests ring as well in the heights of the sky

fairy tale

horned barrels
slay a barefoot echo
ethereal clocks
sneeze in the bottomless pit
solemn thunder sounds at the vault-base
inquisition snakes
are singing in descant
the hypomaniac frogs
shuffle through the cough-syrup

•

a fire-whip cracks
animalistic balls bounce
on the stolen meadows of ermine
on the uppermost twig of the air
sits a tamed egg
which bursts into vivats that find no end
the surging feather-sea
swells in joyful waves
it twitters crows whistles mates trills
as it circles the throne of the star

•

I would rather show you the void
in my sky-blue eyes
than give you the answer
I would rather remove the footman's wool

from the bung-hole of my shame-ladder
made of monomaniac firmament owners

•

then it wanders through billowing forests
and over the leafy sea
peeks out of our knotholes
like a fluorescing skull
and barks at dwarfs

•

meanwhile a worm on a dead-straight road
heads straight for the horizon
according to laws of perspective
the worm should get smaller and smaller
and finally vanish
our worm however gets larger and larger
the further it goes
larger and larger and larger
and finally fills up the cosmos

•

accumulated nightingales
guzzle proclitic moon priamels
in the high-breasted summer night
two milked heroes
march sighing
over a sigh-bridge
two worms with flowing blond curls
follow in adam-attire
and address the two heroes:

do let us come with you
do let us walk the streets for you
retreat down the street
advance up the straight
straight up the straightest of streets
with or without a yardstick
skittle balls in make-up
scurry through the wattles
the game-dice stars
ruffle up their feathers
as if they would like to humour
the abc
of the lordless ladyless bodies

*

in the hollow-cheeked hollowed space of a recess
fireproof goldplated decoys
roll down the unrivalled eloquence-staircase
the catacomb and the catabrush
lie down in their sneeze-caskets
the tables follow the chairs like manikins the ladykins
and what hovers above the tables and chairs in the form
  of a farewell cloud
declares in verse that the situation is hopeless

the roads follow the arrows like the manikins the ladykins
the black knife cuts so deep in our epistle-ring
that as a footnote a chair leg juts out for some footsie
the best it can do is tick yet a bit
and applaud once or twice
the lightning flashes drive the stable-blinded doll carriage
every wheeler-dealer lets himself be crucified
and even caesar hung his bravo by the neck on the
  clothes line
and takes a rest from his napoleon hat

I am a horse

I travel in a train
that is overcrowded
in my compartment
each seat is taken by a woman
with a man sitting on her lap
the air is unbearably tropical
all the travellers have an enormous appetite
they eat without ceasing
suddenly the men
begin to whimper
and long for the maternal breast
they unbutton the women's blouses
and suck the fresh milk to their hearts' content
I alone do not suck
nor am I suckled
nobody sits on my lap
and I'm not on anyone's lap
because I am a horse
immense and upright I sit
with my hind-legs up on the train seat
and comfortably lean
on my fore-legs
I whinny a raucous neigh neigh neigh
on my breast glitter
the sex buttons of sex appeal
in neat little rows
like the glittering buttons on uniforms
oh summertime
oh wide wide world

The Flowersphinx

1

From spider nets the beggars descend. In folds of their black trains they harbour the downy moons stilled lambs flowers without keel or quill and retrieving bats.

From flower pinnacles and the freckled curtains shivering at the breath of the half-wad half-worldly highness the seven barbaric star-brothers draw past.

In secret palm sundays are still taking place. For lack of donkeys the redeemers ride in on tandems.

The king of this city eats rainbows.

2

From the calendar fall the crucified flowers addresses of the long lost and forgotten and cornerstones of royal residences.

In the marble gullet lies the unrolled song-string.

The busts of deceased magnanimous beasts grace the city squares.

Abortions fleshed family trees filled with ingrown erotic boulders shaved steeds and the bags full of flames are carried away in bull-rush baskets.

The thousand towers are made of missals. Into them out of the heavenly beam-straw fall vermin and the peopled worlds.

3

On tortoise shell tracks the maidens glide up. They bear in their aprons the red hot shards of shattered suns.

In great arcs the caryatids of heaven piss forth time like vassalage tributaries.

From the masts of the city glows the great ether medusa. From the vault of her belly sailors have hung homemade pirate galleons en miniature to pass the time of day.

The plant guillotine draws through the street.

The savin mountains have not been sufficiently lowered. The stage wing strings are too short. The jaw of the sistine prayer mill and the lynch gong crowd their way through the crack.

Enormous prophetic globes of black lawn sod hop on the face of the sea.

4

A shaggy star takes a whirl to the aria of a bell.

The flowered runner on which the dream and cloud beasts passed over the mountains is brushed and rolled up.

The carrion balls hung with teeth and wedding rings which I believe to be eagles tainted by ruins are devoured stone weights on the inside of monuments.

The professional lips of the laplanders which I believe to be cooing postal pigeons are carrion balls hung with teeth curls and wedding rings.

The forest is a bellows.

5

In the forests of fleshy family trees the erotic boulders are complaining.

The shaved steeds carry bags full of flames to the crucified flowers.

The lynch gong howls and the jaw of the sistine prayer mill rattles.

Saddled harps fall from the heavenly beam straw.

*

the flowers' piano-pedal is trampled
the ship is unhappy
ever since baby and robin-hood
it has sensed the seeds in its heart
mutating amazons and eggs without throats
threaten its poles
which are marked by foppish urns
if the ship spies brooklets riding on rivers
it barks out its permanent-waves
every ship publishes someday the hundredth edition of its initials
but if all too often it grabs the unworldly kiss by the beard
its air becomes wrinkled
and finally it has to vomit up its rich inner life
then its banners as well are at their last gasp
is this the liquid ruin
the ship carries its drops to the side
and hangs up its continents on coat-hangers
if the ship wags its blood-curdling tail
the circulating music is felt by exhumed virgins
and wenches as dark as ladyships without portholes or hatches
are turned into bedraggled sisters
who even live in the flesh are dead stylish
they take the ship by its rosette-nose
and together they dance the tra-la-la latinate dance
they pull out the staffs from their bars
their antipathy towards funicular numbers is whisked away on the wind

ten-stories they take hold of bell-ropes
with attached equatorial vaticans
they can no longer sense the weight of the spheres and the
feathered singers
with measuring and hot rods they execute
graceful ballet steps and leaps over ribbons
is this the bone-well or the polished-out snout
it is neither
this is the little tree gertrude

*

those were the snakes
monkeys
pianos
with the wild growth under their arms
those were the encapsulated chickens
railroad trains
sailing ships
needles
in the icebound father-land
surrounded by iron of the orchard
in feeble mouths those were
the four-cornered forks
tables
shadows of a fork
that couldn't resist
diving under the table after dinner
to drill between the four table-legs
for tiny four-cornered men
with tiny four-cornered seas in their hands
those were the stags
stepping out of the secretly buried indoor air
who greeted the cats slumbering like snow
riding red dogs
those were the muddled murmuring malformed winds
weather cocks
organ grinders
who lost themselves in the night lights around them
the torn children
scourged dwarfs
naked wet swimmers with book satchels on their backs

trout dressed to dance
those were the ones with the motto of men of the world
float and let float
so-called verse-line tailors from old respectable families
who sank deeper and deeper into thrown-away days
those were the rogues

*

as the floor was removed from under his feet
he fastened himself with his gaze to the ceiling
and saved his shoes
there he hung motionless like a charade sack
addicted to the abc of the lordless ladyless bodies
he felt no compulsion to wipe off a feather shabrack
  hiatus
he strove neither to become a hero of the day nor a hero
  of the night
swamp-medals marsh-scarfs lagoon-beads not even they
  could attract him
he let the volcanoes theodore junior and theodore senior
  smoke to their hearts' content
he let the men stand up like a man
and the women lie down like ladies
at his call salve dust would lie finger thick
if a hieratic quasi-modogeniti
and the patches in his gaze
had not compelled him like an unassuming lorddom
to look over his life unblemished by any patrician felony
  or matrician melony
in the process he let go of his gaze on the ceiling like the
  act of an unspectacled blink-of-the-eye
and as the floor was removed from under his feet
he fell like a confetti cross into the scrubbed-down abyss
  of the void

*

one by one
down goes the unknown flesh
with a dry eye
and breathes
and has a belly in each wrinkle
gradually it learns to say its name
word by word
line by line
because it is flat
and rolls after itself
and suits itself
and understands itself
and always knows itself
up to a wrong plank
three times it knocks against its finger
come in come in come in
there stands the breath-profile
with quicksilver lips
on its tongue
that roll away from under his feet
on four-corner wheels
that turn
when the spokes stop
and stop
when the spokes turn
year by year is years without years
day by day is days without days
the knee boots too walk articulately
through the living flesh-tube
step by step

uninhibited with their annual tree-rings
in well-fitting closely set cages
year by year is years without years

*

there are twenty-four wardrobes
one in each vanilla synagogue of the twenty-four
   continents
in sweden the wardrobe is called a swedish curtain
in spain a spanish screen
in china a chinese wall
in helvetia the bull of uri
if a wardrobe stands on two chair legs
it is a table
waiting on the table are meal-time and grace-time
in the table drawers are alder berries in great profusion
if the table has several drawers
one in each of the three compass directions arp
then it is a railroad train
if the train has a chair-back of blue barrels
that drive a many-saddled angel
one may take a seat
because in this case it is a chair
and won't be leaving
under the chair-seat on a little umbilical cord hangs the
   hoary head
the chair sleeps open-eyed like a hare
therefore one can use the chair to see straight
but a sea level is better
even if the sea rises above it
in well-read circles one likes to ask with a paperweight
   on one's tongue
do you have a comfortable stool
and means in fact the celestial passage
that leads past the genital chamber
into the cloister of warm milk-brothers

at night baby mountain is known as hans
around his jaws fly spineless diamonds
his eyes are wedged between sunrise and sunset
his umbrella handles are budding
when will baby mountain be five

if the trombone bouquets blow brutto netto toot toot
his organs tremble and his governing bodies quake
if the neuter voice cries to the point
the sawdust spills from his bodies
when will baby mountain be five

baby mountain has ten twigs on his ten fingers
baby mountain has two keys on his keyboard
he lets one speak to him play on him
and shoot at his heart and his stars
when will baby mountain be five

once baby mountain is five
he'll get his first wooden shoe clop clop
then he'll hop off in pursuit of shoe number two
that wanders out blithely into the wide world
when will baby mountain be five

in the glass hump a sweet voice is singing

the empty spaces in the marble nests grew larger and larger
and when they were finally full-grown
they wafted sweet fragrance like flowers
and were plucked by the overloads loaded with gold
who took them along to the rose-red offspring
they lay on serpentine paths
and on transparent snakes
and hurled audible shadows into the visible

•

the giant gees arise from their chairs
and chase the little lightning whizes
into the cracks of the air
the giant lightning whizes smash the little gees
gees and lightning whizes tumble pell-mell

•

in the glass hump a sweet voice is singing
yet there is no one at all in the hump
not even a deaf-and-dumb grain of sand
palettes with noses lie on black feathers
and listen with care to the voice
curious blindfolded clouds draw closer
the palettes with noses motion them not to disturb

•

the commas and periods leap into the hat of kisses
and thus escape the hair-raising spring
that rages among the sea-green walking-sticks
caressing stars
light-clad pyramids
quacks cock-a-doodle-do like an elephant
and barks moo like a butterfly

*

the night knits roses on the hem of the fairy tale
the skein of storks fruits pharaoh-harps unravels
death carries its rattling nosegay under the root of the
   void
storks rattle on smoke-stacks
the night is a stuffed fairy tale

the roses stride on porcelain streets and knit from the
   skein of their years one star after another
between the stars a fruit sleeps
empty lands stuffed years laughing suitcases all dance
   together
the storks devour pharaohs
roses grow out of smoke-stacks
death devours one year after another
the pharaohs devour storks
between the fruits a star sleeps. often it laughs softly in its
   sleep like a porcelain harp
rattling fairy tales knitting streets stimulating storks all
   join the dance

growing smoke-stacks devouring harps porcelain nosegays
   are dancing as well
the roots of the pharaohs are made of roses
the storks pack their suitcases full of smoke-stacks and
   exit to the land of the pharaohs

And In Addition

running, leaping dog-paws
and wagging dog-tails
and no dog in between
a stiff little stream
that refuses to end
combed-out forests
lying inert
snakes turned to wax
round as globes
of transparent glass
that quietly roll off
through nature
and in addition blind cows
that speak in blank verse
and out of the water the nudes
who receive now and then
a drop of red ink
from above

*

A stag is rowing his gondola.
Legendarily he shakes his antler-crown
overgrown like a Christmas tree
with rosy-red cheeks
sceptres of glass
rhymed objects.
Before him in the gondol
in a large wicker basket
lies a long black beard
filled with will-o'-the-wisps
tractable lightning flashes
sun-dial petals
tiny spoons that stick out their tongues.
Unfortunately the stag is not able
to mount all his pretty things
in his antler-crown.
But the antlers might still grow
and then each thing
could find its place there.
The stag asks nothing more
than the right to row on undisturbed
and legendarily to shake
his whispering antler-crown.

My Happy Feet

It is evening.
On the eaves of a solitary house
a screech-owl hoots.
It sees death riding up incognito on a bicycle.
Death leans its bicycle
against the wall of the solitary house.
Death is like a white grasshopper.
Soundlessly he jumps through the open window
into the house.
My happy feet don't want to know
what goes on in my heart and my head.
Not even one of their five toes
wants to know.
My happy feet
are especially concerned with properly spreading
each toe that they lift
while they walk.
Now the poor man in the house is finished.
He has been slaughtered already
and his flesh salted down.
I would like a walking-stick
kneaded out of bread.
I would like
a mighty blue-green sea-mouth
with teeth of coral
to crack open the stars
which the sky in the meantime has conjured out.
I would like to be able to crack them like nuts.

Kurt Schwitters *(1887-1947)*

I am went

I whirl-heap.
Wilted winds leaf.
Houses eye men cliffs.
Bevel whirl wind.
Men stone houses cliffs.
Whirl-heap bloods leaf.

The World

poem 2

Houses fall, skies collapse.
Trees tower over trees.
Sky greens red.
Silver fish swim in air.
They are not burned,
So ardent are they.
In eternal silver shines their dawn.
And madness swells up to strut across the sky.
Millions of silver fish are quivering across the distance.
Yet they do not singe their silver wings.
Gently stirs the air with silver wing-beats.
Strut men.
Kneel souls.
Immense across the distance madness grows.

Wheyweight Silverleaf Blossoms

Gleamt beseethe zigzags.
Drizzle-trees piss grimace flowers.
Spring waft torches flamingly.
Sprinkle bladders beefsuet (due to paper shortage).
Nimble legs sulphur arms Marc Chagall.
To me.
To me the fountains.
They flow into themselves and strangle stuck.
You pair to me.
Leaf creep grow flow.
You pair to me.
Your streams glitter thirst.
Misery impregnates sailboats (doll-house-kitchen-fixture-
carton.)
I benight myself.

*To Eve Blossom**

O, thou beloved of my twenty-seven senses, I love thine!
Thou thee thee thine, I thine, thou mine. – We? –
That belongs (by the way) not here.
Who art thou, uncounted woman?
Thou art – art thou? –
The people say thou werst. –
Let them say. They don't know how the churchtower
stands.
Thou wearest thy hat on thy feet and walkest about on thy
hands, on thy hands walkest thou.
Hallo! Thy red dress, shredded into white folds.
Red I love, Eve Blossom, red I love thine!
Thou thee thee thine, I thine, thou mine. – We? –
That belongs (by the way) in the cold fire.
Red Blossom, red Eve Blossom, what do the people say?
Prize-question: *1.*] Eve Blossom is nuts.
2.] Eve Blossom is red.
3.] What colour are the nuts?
Blue is the colour of thy yellow hair.
Red are the kernels of thy green nuts.
Thou simple maiden in everyday-dress, thou sweet green
beast, I love thine! –
Thou thee thee thine, I thine, thou mine. – We? –
That belongs (by the way) in the fire-grate.
Eve Blossom! Eve, E-v-e, I drip thy name.
Thy name drips like soft candle-wax.
Doest thou know, Eve, doest thou already know it?

* This is a second version by Schwitters's son Ernst, in collaboration with Philip and Ursula Granville, of an original translation into English by Schwitters himself of his poem 'Anna Blume'.

One can also read thee from behind, and thou, thou most
glorious of all,
Thou art from the back as from the front: 'E-v-e'.
Candle-wax drips caressing over my back.
Eve Blossom, thou drippy beast, I love thine!

Nights
poem 7

Fervent nights
Blaze anguish
Quivers blaze rapture
Painfully be-oned.
Seething nights lust
Whips fire flash
Flickering dampness.
Could I but bathe the little fish!
Quails a with-in
Quivers un-oned
Lusts damply
Pungent
You
Bride-scent
Roses glow in garden.
Slender spikes fish in whip-air.
Wound knee
Waves surf rapture
Oh, the torment, not to fly!
Rapture over-plunged
Haunts whistle
I yearn your wave
You!
My ardour fevers death
I over-wave
In-jubilant
Whips still fervour.
Over-wells shrill.
Kneels dew on little fish
Little fish legs slide.

White legs has the little fish
White eyes has death!
Blue shines fervent
Hard whips fervent night.
I
Crest-break
Pales tired
Blues anguish sun.

At the edge of my wilting
I am gentle night

Saws knee rain wilt days.
Gentle pious depths gentle hands.
Drip wounded nights nightlong.
Wound gentle giants vault dome.

Evening
poem 25

Glow strokes soft worlds kiss.
Whistle sun thread sun (Zeppelin).
I thread sun glimmer-gloss.
And glimmer-glow softens world.

Golden Stalks

poem 26

Tents have autumned.
Have swans autumned love?
Blaze crumbles corpse-wine.
Thread gleans mosquito dance.
Unitas swans un-dome.
You, Louise!
Blossom bleeds evening stream stalks.
You, Louise!

Green Child

poem 1

Dungeoned air steeps
Murder over-arches blood.
Could I but scherd these walls!
Wall thirsts us.
Oh, this blaze of embracing walls.
Dungeon unites.
Blood dungeons.
Blood steeps –
Vast blood over-arcs.
Run –
Flee –
Fear –
Steeps blood –
Green.
Shot –
Who's shooting? –
Blood?
Brimstone –
Feet over-stumble –
Legs over-race –
Blood –
Fear –
Chase –
Fly –
Scream –
Blood grimaces yellow-hell-yellow –
Yellow-green –
Hell-yellow-green –
Hell-brimstone-yellow-green –
Blood grimaces hell-brimstone-yellow-green.

Could I but wash the green blood!
Wash blood –
Bathe blood –
Blood bath.
Rapturous white blood of my bride!
Green blood steeps –
Screams –
Cheers? –
Schrills –
Be quiet, green-yellow blood!
Brimstone burns green!
I –
Run –
Scream –
My agony I bear on hands –
Like a child –
Now, now don't cry!
Child, dear, green!
It's me, your mother!
Dear child –
Green –
Cries child?
Brimstone-yellow child, how fire-red!
Red –
Blood –
Brimstone-yellow –
Green –
Steeps damnation –
Chase –
Scream –
Torment –
Mad the hunt!
Luck?
Luck! You!

You I love!
You –
White blood, you!
But there steeps!
Brimstone-yellow, green!
Hideously green child.
We run,
On my arm.
Clutch tight!
The walls clutch!
We run walls –
Walls clutch –
They leave me you –
You and I –
Green child –
You and I –
Walls tower –
Blood steeps green.
Walls clutch –
Yellow insight –
Dark red strut –
They would take you! –
No!
Lust alone –
Give back –
Blood-red back –
Green child, how blood red you seem!
Outside black dogs are flying.
Walls tower –
Walls clutch –
I am expecting –
Green child!
Blissful your gaze!
Black dogs fly about the walls –

Green child,
Mine!
Black dogs,
Fly us forth!

Loftiness
poem 8

Churches tower a man.
Burdens sun mountain-chain.
Break through steeply.
Glow runs off intower peaks.
Body-hot: soul-near.
Warmth inblazens blaze.
Small I?
Huge!
Poor I?
Rich!
Weighs mountain-chain,
Weighs giant I!
Blaze man burdens weigh sun.
I?
Inblaze
Steep!

To Johannes Molzahn

Circle worlds you.
You circle worlds.
You overcome twitter Apyl, the machine to waters.
Worlds hurl space.
You hurl worlds space.
Worlds turn the new machine towards you.
To you.
You, yours the new machine space.
And axles break eternity.
The work, to which we, inherited by us, you.

I am constructed

Winch is dawning head laughter.
Deep to inward timid land.
Distant huts are wilting dew.
You.
Meadows bleed mellow snow.
Meadows bleed blood.

Screak

The fish dill screak finger blood.
Mountain-ore mounts mountains.
Tower-high downwards creep your snails.
Loudly darkness divides divisions.
Rings of lead.
Rings of wire.
Snow.
Snow.
Dill are fishing your finger to meet carp-blood.
Still fish dill the screak.
(It is requested that dogs be kept on a leash.)

*

Ice clocks wander alive. On the peak of Mount Simeon, between Berlin and Potsdam, there springs a waterfall. It is a big, beautiful waterfall, such as one usually finds only in the Alps. Its waters splash a sprightly song to the mountain. Day and night, summer and winter, centuries, millennia, hour after hour, it sings the same sprightly song. The breezes over Mount Simeon are washed clean by the water's plunge. It rains snow, and the sun shines. On the slope of the breeze the water is frozen to stone. On the peak the glacier thaws, green is its blood. The breezes are very high, they cannot melt, and daily they are melting, and their waters feed the waterfall. Now, I ask: couldn't someone at least build a power plant up there? This one single waterfall could provide all Berlin with electricity and potatoes.

A Fourth of the Feelings of the Ancient Automato atop his Family Fortress Atho

a romance

Atho
Auto
Automato
The dog oggles gulp at the axis of liqueurs.
Who's been goading on the graters here?
That they all glare against me!
Satyroschematism eyes wink eye.
The calf is dead.
The ladder leans on the hen's behind.
Streetcars drive up and down the ladder.
Wireless.
Poco Sonore.
Automatic.
The dog warms the inner coat.
When the wild wine blooms.
Itch in my left eye.
The calf stays dead.
Bicycle riders are cautioned to remain in their prescribed lanes.

On a Drawing by Marc Chagall

poem 28

Playing-card intones fish, head in the window.
Animal head lusts the bottle.
On hop-skip mouth.
Man without head.
Hand wags sour knife.
Playing-card fish squander dumpling bottle.
And a desk drawer.
Dumb.
And fervently button rounds upon the table.
Fish presses table, stomach sickens sword-strike.
A drunkard stalk blankly eyes the plaintive beast.
Eyes lust deep the bottle's fragrance.

Wire-Circus

Apple skiffs stab eyes. (Eyes front!) humaned bones.
(none that stab.) Humid surge waves humaned wave.
(Stupid question!) Matches here! Acrobats strain arena.
stupidly stares At! (What are you staring?) I humid.
(First prize for fantasy) crocodile whets menagerie.
Wire-tangled eyes warriors. Humans barb wire-welter.
Surge wire-downward. (Mounting of high-voltage
high-wire) creep creep slime commotion. (Charles, the
best snake man as a crocodile.) Human trickleth pig's
knuckle knash spire-wire arena fire-works.
The whole lot of you are ground-floor acrobats!
Surge twittering colossal avalanche. Boom-boom soldiers
wield flog. (Flog-wheel) Flog-wheels lust. (Half-price for
children.) Surges awe silence voices. Human beings
walk two-legged! Humans human. I, too, human. (A bit
of concert orchestra in the arena.)
Humans excluded.
excluded!
Burrow your leg forward. Keep moving, you dog, or I'll
shoot!

It is autumn. Swans devour the bread of their masters
held together by tears. A few feeble expressionists cry
out for wine, for there's still enough wine, but no more
Expressionism.
Long live the Kaiser, for there's no more Kaiser! Clocks
clock the hours 25 thousand times.
I glide.
Glide noose.
Clangs a machine.
Cats hang from the wall.
A Jew is fiddling the beast on out the window.
All the way out.
It is autumn, and the swans autumn also.

The Turning Point

Out of our very own peat-refinery with limited abscission effect in both directions there unmistakably emerges for the expert a double-tongued riddle. Yet the general public maintains, and with a certain semblance of truth, that whatever is right for the expert is not necessarily right in the least for the general public. But the public can, in fact, become too general, and once a certain generality in publication has been overstepped, this claim, in reality, is no longer valid. But as matters happen to stand, it in any case sets itself up for the turning point atop a cherry-chameleon-sour fig tree and shouts halleluja. The well-known jelly-fish is usually yolk yellow, usually, but not always, and out of its eminent funnel result 2 recipients of world-encompassing dimension, somewhat like colophony. Evenings it smiles like wax and drinks ink. Mornings it is as grey as the pitch under a camel's foot. Then it counts twice to 3, up and down the hen-roost, from a hundred to two thousand, back and forth, up and down, down and up again until evening falls and the sheep turn bleating homewards. And the horned bull bellows past all, forcing its way through the stall (see Art Criticism). And the clouds drift on towards the west, come from the west, are wearing vests, and it's raining in the vestibule. The mitten is up overhead, hovering below the clouds in the west, directly above Cape Horn where the sun stands 3 km. beneath the equator and laughs. That I know through personal experience. And the old crone sways to and fro like a milk-pot. She's already 21 and has just had her ninth. Exhausted the bird egg sinks down into the

nest. Bramble berries grow beneath its limbs of far-shadowing birds. In museums they are systematically weaned. Systematic bird collections. Even Tacitus mentions already that birds lay eggs. There are sweet-tasting eggs of sloam and Virginia milk. They're the best of all, as my friend hans arp well knows. For they have 33 (in words, thirty-three) udders each. The udders ring for every season, especially for Christmas and Easter, each one a red rose to the honour of hans arp, the great poet. hans arp is the great egg-udder poet who has unlocked the fountains that the birds may flow forth from their cool tubes. In the course of the May Day demonstration, there was yawning under the ice. The birds then perch sadly beneath the street, the canals (not to be confused with cantalopes or cannibals) have turned sloamy. Becoming becomes and silver-feathered fish swim in the air, somewhat like silicium, not to be confused with Sicily. Great red flags go hungry beneath the grey-historical bankruptcy collections of the neo-capitalists. There are 6 collections. 6 is the only number which, without a second thought, can be stood on its head; 69, in contrast, is fraudulent deception. This fact one can already infer from the servant girls' braids after they have chastely tied on clever blue-striped aprons. For twice wags pigtail behind round the nest on the back of the head wags tail sour cream milk gorge candles prior to briar. 1, 2, 3, 4, 5, 4, 3, 2, 1. 1, 2, 1. 3, 2, 1. 1. *Eight*!
And the moon rages set. – Wait, soon! –

Longing

And
Without
To have
To sing
Earthworm
  To stride
Lyric
Tradition
The beggar
  from
Hollow
Green
By ways of
By the way
The grass

  I don't bother with the ideal.
  I eat the apple with its peal.

Moreover, we know that we must get rid of the idea of 'Art' if we're ever going to reach 'Art'.

Theory of Alternation

Men suffer thousand null.
Pardon sink poison shadows.
Pardon depths.
Pardon stars heaven.
Suffer depths thousand null.
Suffer thousand.
Over.

The most important aspect of education is the example.
Without it all teaching and encouragement is to no avail.

SADDLE AND TAPESTRY JOURNAL

The Hand

I am the hand.
The hand is the man.
The man is the hand.
The earth is the world.
We men are great.
Never do men overbear over.
I am the hand.
Never do hands overbear over.

You

My sing is empty
Screaming yawns.
Screaming broadens,
Bellows yawn broadens;
I pungent you.
I pungent your breath.
I sing your eyes.
Your striding yearns my eyes.
Your chatting yearns my ear.
I thirst aroma the hours
You are my yearning.
You are your striding, your eyes, your prayer.
Your laughter prays,
Your chatter prays,
Your eye prays.
My yearning distants your praying scream.
I
Distant you.

Ice Clocks

Simmer clocks simmer breathe ice
Blaze crumples blaze simmer ice
Clocks cook clocks ice seethe blaze
Clocks cook ice
Mimose, Orange, Aphrodite, Tulip Flora, Aphrodite.
I wander alive a dead fish.

The Meadow

The meadow grows. Woe to him who harbours meadows within. How can the meadow grow? I can't see how it could grow. Nor can the great arp. Grass grows blades. The meadow raises up blades to the sky. The wind stirs winds. Blade quivers desire. The sun illuminates grass. The sun mirrors off my blue. And earth-smell wafts over. Who can growth?
Who can know the meadow? I dream meadow (pra)

Murder Machine

Welcome, 260 thousand cubic centimeters.
I yours.
You mine,
We me.
And sun eternity glitter stars.
Suffering suffers dew.
Oh, woe you me!
  Memorandum:
5,000 mark reward!
A crate is crooked, especially your crate.
There is no more property, only communism still
    acknowledges property.
I wilt the reed, for there is no more reed.
I leaf the clock, for there is no more clock.
1, 2, 3, 4, 5, 6, seven.
Sunday greens warmth.
The elephant.
The fat elephant.
In case more than one person should lay claim to the
    reward, we shall retain the rights of distribution
    admitting of no appeal.
The magistrate of the royal capital and residence.

I. V. Weber

Speechless

A worm hangs from a hook on the line.
A fish bites the worm.
The fish bites the hook as well.
The line pulls the fish.
Now the fish hangs on the line.
The line pulls it up in the air.
The fish dies in the air.
The line dies the fish.
A new worm hangs on the line.
A new fish bites the new worm.
And from out of the ruins, new life flowers forth.

Village

From the roadside ditch a sweet bramble-berry ripens
  towards me.
Milk is the smile of sleep, pious and good.
In the middle of the town stands a mottled cow.
In the midst of the middle stands a man.
The mailbox hangs on the house.
Wire is the soul of electricity.
The woman shrieks 'ua i au'.
'Baa' says the sheep.
The girl is wearing an apron.
The naked foot, too, belongs to the girl.
Along the bee-fence stands Bluma Anna.

Cigarren

[*elementary*]

Cigarren
Ci
garr
ren
Ce
i
ge
a
err
err
e
en
Ce
CeI
CeIGe
CeIGeA
CeIGeAErr
CeIGeAErrEr
CeIGeAErrErr
CeIGeAErrErr
ErrEEn
EEn
En
Ce
i
ge
a
err
err
e
en
Ci
garr
ren
Cigarren

[The last verse to be sung.]

Register
[*elementary*]

Z
A R P
A B C
D E F
G H I
K L M
N O P Q
R S T V
A B C
T U V W
W V U T
Z
X Y Z
Z
Z
Z

Composed Picture Poem

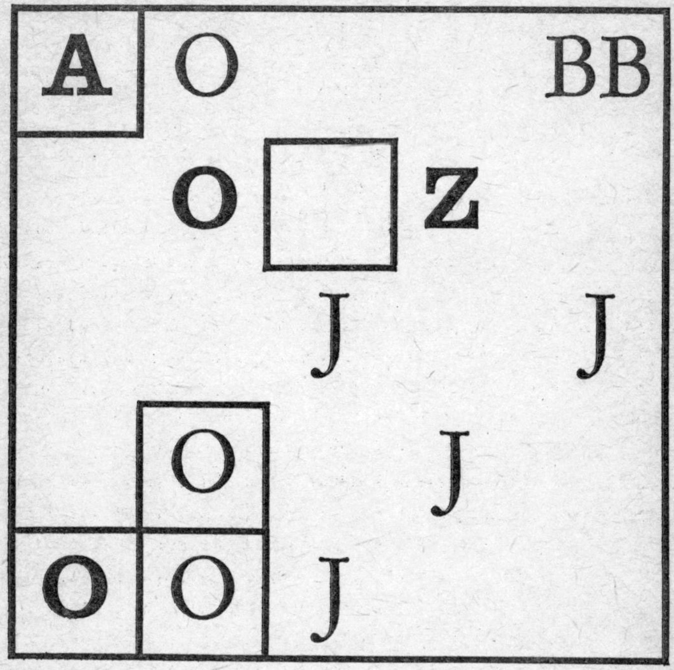

Poem 25

[*elementary*]

25
25, 25, 26
26, 26, 27
27, 27, 28
28, 28, 29
31, 33, 35, 37, 39
42, 44, 46, 48, 52
53
9, 9, 9
54
8, 8, 8
55
7, 7, 7
56
6, 6, 6
56
6, 6, 6
¾6
57
5, 5, 5
⅔5
58
4, 4, 4
½4
59
4, 4, 4
½4
25
4, 4, 4
½4
4, 4, 4
½4
4, 4
4
4
4

Z A
[*elementary*]

Z Y X
W V U
T S R Q
P O N M
L K I H
G F E
D C B A

The Onion

Merz Poem 8

It was a most eventworthy day, the day on which I was to be butchered. (Fear not, have faith!) The king was ready, the two seconds were waiting. The butcher was scheduled for half past six: it was already six fifteen, and I myself was supervising the necessary preparations. The platform we had chosen was spacious, so that numerous spectators could participate in a maximum of comfort. There was a telephone within easy reach. The doctor lived in the house next door and was standing by in case any of the spectators should faint. (Reminiscent of confirmation.) Two immense block and tackle hung suspended from the ceiling to hoist me up afterwards in case I were to be disembowelled. Four hefty workmen were also present to lend a hand, former Russian prisoners of war, with rugged, raw-boned frames. (Journal for Home and Property Owners.) Two spotless maids had taken their place, dazzling young lasses. It was comforting to think that these two pretty girls would whisk my blood and wash and lay out my inner organs. The platform was swept and scrubbed. I had specified that two long tables, scoured white, be placed along a side wall: on them stood an assortment of bowls, knives and forks. I had just requested that a wash-basin, water and a towel be brought, also a piece of soap (Sunlight). Anna and Emma, the two maids, brought in a tub and a wooden beater. It's a funny feeling – that one is about to be butchered in ten minutes' time. (The sacrifice of motherhood.) Up to now, I'd never in all my life been butchered. One must first be ripe for the occasion. For, as a rule, it's when the potatoes have to come out and the oats are all gone that hard times have truly begun. We've yet to have any real summer this year. Ten minutes can seem an eternity. (Faith, hope and charity.) (Ducks goose in the meadow.) Everything had been prepared, down to the last detail. The princess was already making her entrance. She wore a short, white skirt, a bit rumpled from sitting, but particularly flattering for just that reason. The church spire, after all, is very steep. Spring meadow, dedicated in friendship. Delicately hops fidget king's daughter little legs. I adore these delicate fidget hop-king-daughter-little-leglets. Tail wags sour cream. She stood inkwell before me and asked bell-pure lace-white, 'Are you to be butchered today?' Fish hot knives shoot blood. I lowered purple eyes and was happy at her greeting. 'How handsome you are, Alves Groomstick, such a handsome man,' said she red lips vein boil blood, bon voyage! pert thread-point nose: 'I bring to you your last greeting from the world. Get thee to a nunnery. (My house, thy world.) (Headless leather.) Felt according to navel size. You must be in a bit of a hurry these days getting everything ready for this solemn event. (Peace be with you.) How quickly you've ripened, yes, overripened! With what joy you may gaze upon your ripeness. May it always bring you nothing but happiness. How fortunate, that the weather has held for your slaughter-day and that the butcher will be able to come on his bicycle.' (Genuine Brussels Handwork.) Good health is fortune's gift. 'Would you excuse me, little Princess, while I make a phone call? It's already six thirty, and the butcher still hasn't come.' 'Hello, is this the butcher? The crowd is getting restless, what's holding you up?' (From now to eternity!) 'Go ahead and begin the formalities. I've just this moment finished impaling my sister on the church spire as a weathercock. The

church spire, after all, is very steep, and overhead fish spikes in whip-air. The lightning rod was rusty, and I had trouble forcing it through my sister's tummy. Yet bright spikes fish in whip-stench. Begin the ceremony!'
I called for the king; 'Into thy hands, oh Majesty, I commend my comely form. My corpse, oh King, at thy disposal!' (The millimetre line divided by six costs 20 pfennig.) The king gave a signal. (Fortuna Whetmachine.) The two seconds in black frock coats and black gloves, top-hats and black cravats took their positions at the king's side. A black dog flew past cawing. The king gave another signal. The four Russians and Anna and Emma made ready to be of assistance. Again the king signalled. The seconds approached, introduced themselves and asked if I had any last requests. (Lift up your eyes to the star!) I requested that the princess sing the International and then afterwards give me a kiss. (Unheaded necks, genuine cowhide.) A lady in the king's retinue fell unconscious to the floor. The doctor was summoned. Firmly whips ardently. The princess sang:

'Worker trumpets
C sharp D
D sharp E flat
sharp E
you yours your you,'

the entire International. Lamp-post trumpets kiss full skirts surge white lace kiss. Sling arms full skirts surge neck lace warm tubes smooth sleek fish carp, carp, carp. (Prière de fermer la porte.) Do shut the door, yes, you, you, you! I love you so! (The world with all its sins.) Now – butcher me!
The king signals again, the butcher rides up. Not a sound in the house. Pro patria est, dum ludere videmur.

(Red-yellow-blue lady battalion.) (No smoking, likewise no holding-in-the-hand of unlit cigars.) Two workmen lead off his bicycle. (Sacrifice for God and country.) A workman brings a club, big balloon lemon-pale. (Hold on to what you've got.) The butcher has a blue-striped apron flutter rag. (Sugar-beet girl.) October inclines ceremony rivals seconds. – Begin! – And me, like a hedgehog! – The butcher leans back, head tilted, club raised. (The brightest jewel, the highest joy, a familiar touch of home.) The butcher springs forward. (This is love!), swings club sink sink weight weight weight, fervently whips sink weight weight wait wait wait. – My skull shattered.

Now it was time for me to collapse, so I collapsed lapsed lapsed lapsed, flat. Aaaaa aaaaaaa aaa aaaaa b. (Applause from all pews.)

What next? My arms and legs were tied to winches, winches winch up. Sink slings flat together spread apart. (A call to all hand and head workers.) My side was pierced. Blood bucked bucket blue ray red thick whip. Beat maids beater together rack railroad train machines beat Emma Anna. (Blameless, you have committed your heart today to the holy bond.) The king commanded a drink. Blue scorched flame murder gravely gravely. Empty burns the stomach flame sulphur blood. From that moment on the king has had no beard. Be steadfast in duty, stand fast. (Contributed by the editorial staff.) There is a science to everything. (Amplification, Soviet Association for Capitalistic Construction, Berlin.) Now I was to be disembowelled. (Freshest mocca bonbons, freshness.) Transfers drive knives slit quiver entrails. (Peacetime commodities.) It was a most eventworthy garden restaurant. I felt a thousand joys, rescuer tomorrow twenty. Three lustrums only did the glass-house bred specimen blossom. (Roar of applause.) Moon calf shines inside gently tugged entrails unstunned. (All for the Red Army.) Clean, clean, be clean my girls, clean in washing, that nothing burn. (God protect you.) (God protect you.) Flame hot, flame hot! Earthworms played gently within my belly; it tickled slightly. The king yearned my eyes. Have brought to me, daughter of the king, the eyes of John the Baptist! (Today you shall quit your father's house.) Round globes slick slime writhing sprang from the eyes towards gentle hands. On a plate, knife and fork the eyes were served. (Hard-of-hearing and deafened soldiers to receive, without charge, advice and information.) Slick slimed oyster eyes sink stomach heavily. Children under twelve admitted only under surveillance and in the company of adults; in addition, children under eight to be held by the hand on request. (Entrance fee 50 pfennig, but at least one mark.) 'Poison!' shrieked the king, writhing on the floor. (The role of the cradle in populating the world.) 'Sweet dreams, I've been poisoned.' (August has 31 days, the days subtract an hour and 56 minutes.) Yes, how awful. 'In you, oh Lord, I trust. I lift up my hands.' Two mushrooms grew up eyes stem smooth bumps milk and drilled two holes in the king's belly. Stem-eyed eyed eyes. Silent startled king's chalk. The princess's heart was pounding fiercely. (Acetylene does away with the odour of bodily secretions.) She felt so sorry for her father. The doctor was summoned to do something about the holes in the king's stomach. (Veritas vincit, with Anna Blume in the leading role.) The old king had fainted. Fear peaks silver strings stone to stone. The princess gave a signal ordering that I be put back together again. (It is in this manner that bed feathers are cleaned, dusted, washed, steamed and dried.)

They began to reassemble me. First, with a gentle shove, my eyes were pushed back into their sockets. (Fear not: faith, hope and charity are the stars.) Next, someone brought my inner parts. Fortunately, they hadn't yet been boiled or chopped up into sausage. (Vaincu mais non dompté.) And yet one is willing to settle for a beautiful autumn. Thanks to my own inner magnetic currents, my inner parts, the moment they were inserted, sprang back into place and took root where they belonged. (How to achieve happiness in marriage.) There were certain difficulties to be overcome in ordering the entrails, as they had been somewhat scrambled in all the excitement. (Saint Florian has moved his act to the German stage. A smash hit every evening.) But I realized what was wrong and directed my magnetic currents back and forth, to and fro, one two one two one the tone rumple beams in the eye. I pulled and tugged magnetically at the entrails until they all lay safely in their accustomed place. In this undertaking, I was greatly aided by my knowledge of the inner man. (One year trial period, then permanent appointment as a Prussian civil servant.) Yes indeed! My permanent parts, in the meantime, had been reassembled, and now all that was missing was my blood. (Bordens sweet milk chocolate.) The maids held the bowl of blood beneath the wound in my side and beat in the opposite direction. The king gave a loud moan. By means of my magnetic currents a thick stream of blood lifted itself up from the red surface and entered the wound in my side. (Facts that every woman has to know one mustn't reveal to a girl.) Slowly my veins filled, my heart was full, my inner parts absorbed the blood. But my heart had not yet stirred, I was still dead. (Wet Paint.) The butcher touched the wound in my side with the knife, plunged it in deep and then withdrew it, and – the wound was closed! (Detach here and return to above address.) Every woman should take pains, after the marriage ceremony at least, to inform herself about these matters. I now had all my parts back together again: there were only a few scattered holes where tiny scraps of flesh had clung to the knife. The desire and the need are at hand, all that is lacking is the occasion. There was also a considerable amount of blood lacking, as the king had drunk it all. (For the ideals of Socialism.) Ever since I've been somewhat anaemic. Take the cage home and buy yourself a bird. Hoists were lowered hoist pulleys upwards. Now I could sense that it was time for me to straighten up, so I straightened up, quickly at first, then more and more slowly, until finally I was standing. (Grumbling now, my heart and mouth.) In the land of the Burgundians, there dwelt a fair young maid: I'm nothing but a woman. Remember, my child, where it is you are going. Grow up to be pious and good. Stay pious, my child. Embark boldly on the journey of life. (Vote socialistic!) Ceremoniously the two seconds assumed their positions at my side and took my hands. (Preparation of all prescriptions covered by health insurance policies.) Childhood days were at an end, now life's battle must begin. I was very curious to see how they planned to bring me back to life again. (Ism-sorter by Jefim Golycheff.) It is strictly forbidden to touch objects in the collection. I felt dizzy. (Strindberg quietly undermine Stramm.) Our dear old teacher always liked to season his lectures with a touch of humour, and rightly so. (Sunray.) I don't believe in anything at all. (Trombone festival.) Your guess was right! Appeal in trying times to bible-toting, evangelical school marms. (Everything that the man should know about pregnancy and childbirth!) Your mouth is a saw. (Dentist sunshine.) The butcher again took up his club (the tragedy of becoming human), stood before me (the conduct of the husband during pregnancy), and gently laid the club against my split skull. (Yet Rudolf Bauer *is* an artist.) Anna Blume wait lilac blue roses shoot spike gaps lunk-lump bed. (Ripe for the plucking, fervently one.) A partial explanation misses the mark. Then the butcher leapt back with a mighty bound. (The colonel is and will remain a gentleman, even if he's an idiot!) The woman must know all. There was an ear-splitting crack as the club sprang loose from my skull. The means hereto are offered by a work intended for women readers only. Table of Contents: 1. How to win love. 2. The tamed shrew. 3. What girls like in a man. 4. Something about kissing. 5. How to make an impression. 6. On being turned down. 7. Is misogamy justified? 8. Causes of chastity. 9. Older opinions. 10. How to attain moderation. 11. Good advice. 12. Is love blind? 13. How to recognize true love. 14. The husband's premarital past. 15. The most intimate of intimacies. 16. The new faith. 17. The dark star. The butcher sprang back into his original starting position. (He shall be your lord and master.) The mainstay of the firm, however, remains chaste and pure. (Jamais embrassé.) The fragments of my skull flew together; I was, so to speak, back in one piece again. (Sweet moment.) You ain't et your fritters and the pickles is too greasy. The theatre, as a matter of fact, exists solely for humans who, in fact, are inhuman. (Delivery on receipt of payment; the book is richly illustrated.) It was an odd sensation – being alive again. Selzer-water sails illumine fragrance Maria. I felt that I should strike a pose, so I struck a pose. (The king had just died.) With a grand gesture I approached the king's daughter and wordlessly gave her my hand. (Kiss me!) The king's daughter fell down before me on her pretty, pointed knee. (From one's most immediate childhood surroundings.) Meanwhile, the doctor was knashing pickled pig's knuckles. (See supplement for further announcement of positions open.) She implored me now to save her father. (Happiness in the cottage on the heath.) I realized that in this matter I could not afford to be kind-hearted; kind-heartedness is the mark of a fool. (Anna Blume remains severe.) (The dangerous age.) 'Your father,' I said, 'the king, the king will stay dead.' (Slip-leather of sealskin.) The doctor had fainted away. I arranged for two yellow wax candles to be placed in the holes in the king's belly and then lighted. (Stamps will be accepted in payment.) As the flames licked through the holes, the king exploded. The people below, however, broke out into cheers on my behalf. (The meaning of Socialism is work!)

Paul Klee *(1879-1940)*

*

Animals more grand mourn at the table
that they haven't had enough.
But the clever little flies
climb about on Bread-Mountain
and dwell in Butterville.

•

One thing alone is true
In the 'I', a weight, a small stone.

•

One eye that sees,
another, that feels.

•

Man-beast
Clock of blood.

•

The moon
in the train station: one of many lamps
in the forest: a drop in the beard
on the mountain; see that it doesn't roll,
that the cactus not spear it,
that you not sprinkle the bladder.

*

Open up, you cavern gate,
Earth-dungeon, set me free!
Yield up this inkling of illumination.
And bright hands come to hold me,
and a friend's words joyfully say:
Come forth, you images of beautiful, wild beasts,
emerge now from your prison-keep,
that your fingers may gently glide
through flaming fur,
and man again be one, as once
in God's garden.
Day and night
and sun and splendour of the stars.

– In the paradise of poetry – trembling –

*

There exist two mountains
where all is bright and clear,
one is the mountain of animals,
the other, the mountain of gods.
But between the two there lies
the dusky valley of men.

If anyone looks upward
he is struck by a presentiment
of some insatiable longing,
he, who knows he does not know,
towards those not knowing that they know not
and towards those who know that they know.

*

Your head is a tower
with beam-dancing lens.

•

The practised hand often
knows it better than the head.

•

Oh poet!
If you wish to depict the mould of a tomb,
and you falter for lack
of much-needed inspiration,
go buy yourself a camembert,
and you'll be able at least
to take a good whiff now and then.

*

What does the artist form?
Spaces and shapes!
How does he form them?
In chosen proportions . . .

oh, satire,
bane of intellectuals.

Language without Reason

– Reason swam forth on the river of wine –

A good fish haul is consolation.

2
Meanness is trying to steal up on me
this year as well.

3
Something has to save me.
Success?

4
Inspiration: does it have eyes,
or is it sleep-walking?

5
Now and then my hands lie folded.
Yet just below, the stomach digests
and the kidneys filter bright urine.

6
To love music above all else
means unhappiness.

7
Twelve fish,
twelve dead.

Herr Waldemar,
as the carrion fly
settled on his hand:

'A bit more patience,
if you please!'

Satirical Opus

The happy man, a half idiot,
for whom everything flourishes
and bears fruit.
Standing on his little acre,
one hand clasps the watering can,
the other points at himself,
the navel of the world.

Everything blossoms and thrives,
fruit-laden branches bend down upon him.

*

Because I came, blossoms opened.
Abundance all around, because I am.
Spellbound my heart, my ear
to nightingales.
Father I am to all,
of all on stars
and in the furthermost distance.
And
because I went, the evening fell
and cloud-robes
shrouded light,
because I went
the void cast shadows
over all.
Oh
you thorn
in the silver swelling fruit.

*

Now the departure will sound completely different:

I grew up alone on the heath.
Who has ever helped me?
Storms came and went,
swept away whatever was weak.
I remained on the heath.

Then you came and sought refuge beside me.
But Fate forbad us a hold.
In solitude, your strength, spoke Fate.
My refuge be in thought alone.

*

I well know
the harp-like art
of inward resonance.

And I'm acquainted with
the ethos
appropriate to such spheres.

Equally well I know
music's realm of pathos,
and can contrive for it with ease
an appropriate visual analogue.

But at the moment
I have no need for either.
To the contrary,
I should be as simple
as a little folk song:
artlessly sensual,
open-eyed.

Ethos may wait
at a distance.
There's no hurry.

Pathos can be
overcome.
Why the rush to leave
a joyful this-worldliness?

The only problem:
to make up for developments,
already past,
but 'one must!'

*

The retrospective view at the end of the year
should perhaps be taken more seriously than before.

It's not such a harmless pass-time
to bring children into the world.

Bluish across the horizon,
phosphorescing sheet-lightning.

I, as actor, with folded arms
at the centre of the circle:
'Let it lightning!'

The pose, meanwhile, didn't last long.
One becomes, in the course of one day,
for a while, a bit larger,
and then a bit smaller again.

Something of the spirit
of Joseph the carpenter
is also appropriate
to such a small-scale patriarch.

Something of the sublimity,
something of the pretension,
something of the bizarre,
something of the spiritual,
all lying under lock and key.

*

Grandpapa rides the merry-go-round astride the pepper -
mill.
A thief? Quick, some teeth for the dog!

You'd like?
A crystal ball!
How large?
Perhaps in full-moon size!
– Smile of mutual comprehension. –

Not everyone should decipher this,
else, alas
I'd be totally betrayed.

*

Flesh of the flesh
this man disdains to devour.
He would smell it instead,
thereby
remaining pure
and too great a coward
to act.

*

Little birds are lucky:
they're able
not to think of trunks and roots
and nimbly swing, so self-content,
and all day sing
from tips
of new-branched twigs.

I am God

So much of the godly
is gathered in me
that I cannot die.

My head glows to the point of bursting.

One of the worlds that it harbours
demands to be born.

But now I must suffer
in the act of fulfilment.

*

Depart, you grand desires,
Immortality, farewell.
Flatten mountains of the spirit,
When loneliness is the peak.

*

No one need be ironical about me.
I see to that myself.

I dreamt that
I slew a young man
and called him an ape as he died.
The man was offended,
he was, after all, almost dead.

So much the worse for him
I replied,
no chance for him now to evolve,

to surmount the plump bourgeoisie.

Dream

I am visiting a magician
who receives me in his garden.
He shows me to a bench
made of crimson roses.
Please!
Do be seated –
I do as if.
He sits down on the bench without batting an eye.
My mock stance becomes more and more awkward.
Vis-à-vis at the window
stands the magician's daughter.
I smile up at her, embarrassed.
Enraged, she slams the window
but, from behind the curtains,
continues to watch me
more unabashedly than before.

In dreams there often return
moments from life
that surprised us and
for an instant
left us helpless.
Usually they are petty.
Strong impressions
in which one mastered oneself
remain distant.

*

It was a seductive water
that lured my mind into its curling whirlpool.
But how violent now
the current's force.
Once known places calling past me, traces
of ancient, dark-sweet home
where nights, alone
and covert,
I listened to the cicada's song
beneath the sweet-scented elder-berry tree.
Many sad faces I see along the banks.
But I ride abreast the waves,
strong and fresh in body and soul.
I must meet the great river.
Into the river I must flow.

*

Water,
topped by waves,
topped by a boat,
topped by a woman,
topped by a man.

Dream

I discover my house: empty,
drunk up, the wine
drained off, the stream
pilfered, my barest essentials –
effaced, the epitaph.
White in white.

*

Woe to me
beneath the burden of the recurrent hour,
alone in the centre
in the depths, the slithering worm.

•

A flash in the night:
Strident, the day cries out in its sleep.
Mr Eye-Tooth Heel
who by Mrs Peal
has been invited
to a full meal.

The Epigone

There flows in me the blood of a better era.
Sleepwalking through the present
I cling to my home of the past,
to the grave of my homeland.
For earth devoured all.
The southern sun does not ease my suffering.

*

For such states
there are suitable cures.
Prayers for faith
and for strength.
Goethe's *Voyage to*
Italy belongs here, too.

But, above all, a lucky
star. I've often seen it.
I'll find it again.

*

The storm sets powerful thighs
into the trough of waves
and into the neck of oaks.
It looks like a fight
between spindrift and branch
and yet is a game.
A deity is there
to mark the boundaries.

*

Notes from the distance.
Early morning and
a friend behind the mountain.
Horn-tone,
emeralds.

Thought greeting hails me.
Promising kiss of expectant souls.
It was a star that bound us,
its eye had found us.

Two 'I's as content
thus more than mere vessel.
Sacred stones yesterday,
today, without enigma.
Today, Sense!

Early morning
and a friend behind the mountain.

*

You should pray:
let my soul forget
that it errs.

If pain would change you,
into a beast, at least,
red cloth
around the throat –
you stupid smiler,
rosy smiles.

*

My crystal-clear soul, but
here and there, breath-fogged,
and often clouded, my towers.

Pain sat down with love
and without yearnings
I can live neither
long nor briefly.

*

Farewell, life that I lead
at the present.

You're going to have to change.
Elegant you were,
pure intellect,
quiet and solitary.

Farewell, honour,
at the first public step.

*

I'm
now
thirty years old.
That's a bit of a shock.

'Let it have been,
your dreams,
fantasies.
– The new formula –
to be as one can be.
Realpolitik itzo
and no more spiralling
wingèd ascents.'

But the vagabond remains
incorrigibly
confident.

*

Little rogue on my lips.
Your time is up.
We were comrades,
now our friendship is dust.

I've acquired a piece of heaven,
there I've need of no one
from this world.
Those who scoff –
          they say I'm in love –
remain below and grow old.

Up above we draw
the first circles
of immortality.

Three Boys

The first:

The birds I shoot in flight.
The bow I cut myself.
Proud I am of this art.

The second:

Last spring it leapt into my arms.
I felt that I should embrace.
A gentle yearning set me adrift with the clouds.
Why do tears rush to my eyes?

The third:

This was no winsome girl.
It was a woman, almost as strong as I.
And as I seized her,
I felt the throb of hot blood.
Her breath singed my face.
And with her my whole being glowed with the release
that comes from woman.

*

What I am – do not ask.
I am nothing,
I stand for nothing.
I know nothing but my own happiness.
Whether I have earned it – do not ask.
Simply accept
that it is rich and profound.

Before sunset I should have reached my goal.
Beside her.
I had kept a good pace,
but I had miscalculated.
An ineffable longing towards my goal
burdened the many hours.
A wild pass I must cross
into the mild valley.

*

Sensuality
is the pliability of flesh
under a higher stress.
Eyes blinded by colour,
ears bathed in sound,
noses in scents.
Likewise the organs of love.

Reduction!

One would like to say more
than nature
and makes
the impossible mistake
of wanting to say it
with more means
rather than fewer.

Light
and the rational forms
exist in continuous struggle.
Light sets them in motion,
bends straight lines
makes ovals of parallels
turns circles in intervals
activates the intervening space.

Thus the inexhaustible
multiplicity.

*

Genesis, as formal movement, is the essence of a work.
In the beginning, the motif, intervention of energy, sperma.
Works as form-building in the material sense: primordially feminine.
Works as form-determining sperma: primordially masculine.
My drawings belong to the masculine realm.

*

Form construction
is diminished in energy
in contrast to form determination.

The final consequence of both means of forming
is form itself.

From paths to the goal.

From act to Perfectum.

From state of change
to final state.

In the beginning
the masculine speciality
of the energetic shove.

Then the corporal growth of the egg.

Or:
first the lightning flash,
then the raining cloud.

Where is the spirit the purest?
In the beginning.

Here work that is becoming,
two-part.
Here work that is.

*

On every hand and foot
On every hand and leg

W INTEREST S

Beggar-poor and rich

An AMME sandwiched in between
CA and EL
Whereby one M without doubt
One could easily leave out.